VOLUNTEERING FOR
ANIMAL WELFARE

by Walt K. Moon

BrightPoint Press

San Diego, CA

BrightPoint Press

© 2022 BrightPoint Press
an imprint of ReferencePoint Press, Inc.
Printed in the United States

For more information, contact:
BrightPoint Press
PO Box 27779
San Diego, CA 92198
www.BrightPointPress.com

LIBRARY OF CONGRESS CATALOGING-IN-PUBLICATION DATA

Names: Moon, Walt K., author.
Title: Volunteering for animal welfare / by Walt K. Moon.
Description: San Diego, CA : BrightPoint Press, [2022] | Series: Get involved | Includes
   bibliographical references and index. | Audience: Grades 7-9
Identifiers: LCCN 2021007415 (print) | LCCN 2021007416 (eBook) | ISBN 9781678201265
   (hardcover) | ISBN 9781678201272 (eBook)
Subjects: LCSH: Animal welfare--Juvenile literature. | Volunteer workers in animal shelters--
   Juvenile literature. | Young volunteers--Juvenile literature. | Voluntarism--Juvenile literature.
Classification: LCC HV4708 .M667 2022 (print) | LCC HV4708 (eBook) | DDC 636.08/32--
   dc23
LC record available at https://lccn.loc.gov/2021007415
LC eBook record available at https://lccn.loc.gov/2021007416

CONTENTS

AT A GLANCE   4

INTRODUCTION   6
A DAY AT THE SHELTER

CHAPTER ONE   12
HOW CAN I VOLUNTEER
AT AN ANIMAL SHELTER?

CHAPTER TWO   28
HOW CAN I VOLUNTEER
AT A WILDLIFE CENTER?

CHAPTER THREE   44
HOW CAN I VOLUNTEER
AS A CITIZEN SCIENTIST?

CHAPTER FOUR   60
HOW CAN I VOLUNTEER AT A ZOO?

Glossary   74
Source Notes   75
For Further Research   76
Related Organizations   77
Index   78
Image Credits   79
About the Author   80

AT A GLANCE

- People can volunteer for animal welfare by helping at animal shelters, at wildlife centers, as citizen scientists, and at zoos.

- Animal shelters take care of stray and lost pets, helping them find homes. Volunteers may feed animals, do laundry, and socialize animals. They may also use their skills in social media, writing, or photography to help the shelter.

- Wildlife centers care for wild animals that are injured, sick, or orphaned. Volunteers take care of animals, do laundry, and support the veterinary staff at the center. They may get the chance to release the healed animals back into the wild.

- Citizen science is when everyday people get involved in collecting data for scientific projects. Volunteers in citizen science projects can help observe local wildlife, such as birds, frogs, and other species. This work can help scientists with conservation efforts.

- People visit zoos across the nation and around the world. In addition to professional zookeeping staff, these places use many volunteers. Volunteers help guests find their way around the zoo. They also educate guests about animals and conservation efforts.

- Volunteering with animals has many benefits. Many people enjoy spending time with animals. Volunteers gain useful skills and experience. They may learn about a future career. They get a chance to demonstrate responsibility and help animals locally and around the world.

A DAY AT THE SHELTER

Sofia pulled open the front door, passed through the lobby, and walked into the animal shelter. Down the hallway in a separate room, cats looked around cautiously through glass windows. Sofia smiled. It was time for another volunteer shift at the shelter. She had just turned

There are many animal shelters across the United States. They need volunteers, including people who can help train animals.

sixteen, so she could now volunteer without

adult supervision.

Sofia used the volunteer computer to sign in. Today she would be working with cats, then running some laundry. The cats were in a room with a large common area. Some were walking around. Others were sound asleep. Sofia sat with the cats and petted some of them. By doing this, she was helping the cats get used to humans. This would make it easier for the cats to find homes. After she was done, she was sure to sanitize her hands. Sofia did not have a cat of her own yet, but she hoped to convince her parents soon.

Some shelters have a large room where several cats can stay.

Next it was off to the laundry room. Animal shelters go through lots of laundry. Blankets are used for bedding. Towels are used for cleaning up. Sheets are hung to give shy animals privacy. Sofia collected the dirty laundry from around the shelter.

There are many ways to help animals in need.

Then she filled the industrial-sized washing

machines and got them started.

   Sofia's three-hour shift went by in a flash.

She loved the feeling of helping animals.

She was already looking forward to her

next shift.

PEOPLE HELPING ANIMALS

Helping at animal shelters is a common way people volunteer with animals. But there are also other ways to get involved. People can volunteer at wildlife rehabilitation centers. They can help out through citizen science. They can volunteer at zoos too.

Volunteering with animals can be fun and rewarding. Volunteering can help people learn about different careers. They can learn new skills. Volunteering is valuable on applications for jobs or colleges. For animal lovers, being able to work with animals may be enough of a reward by itself.

CHAPTER ONE

HOW CAN I VOLUNTEER AT AN ANIMAL SHELTER?

Animal shelters are places that care for animals and work to find homes for them. People may drop off a pet at a shelter if they are unable to care for it. The shelter may take in stray or lost animals. It may also take in animals that have been

Animal shelters take in unwanted, mistreated, or stray animals.

mistreated. Shelters most commonly care for dogs and cats. But some take in other kinds of animals too, such as rabbits, snakes, or birds.

Shelters vary widely. Some are made up of one or two rooms and a handful of **kennels**. Others are large, fancy facilities.

They may play calming music to reduce

stress for both animals and people. They

may have features like fountains and pet

supply shops to attract visitors.

Different shelters vary in how they are

run. Some are run by local governments.

SHELTER OR RESCUE?

Animal shelters and animal rescues have similar
missions. But they work differently. Animal
shelters usually have their own buildings. A
lot of people take care of the homeless pets
and find people to adopt the animals. Animal
rescues are usually based in one or more
homes. The animals live with foster families.
Rescues search for people who are a good fit to
adopt the animals.

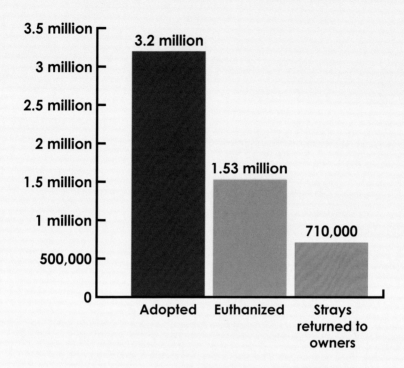

SHELTER ANIMAL STATISTICS

Source: "Pet Statistics," ASPCA, 2021. www.aspca.org.

A lot of dogs and cats end up in animal shelters each year. This graph shows the yearly estimates of various outcomes for those dogs and cats from 2015 to 2018.

They usually take in all the animals that come to them. Some of these shelters must **euthanize** animals to make room for others. Other shelters are nonprofit organizations. They rely on donations. They may be no-kill shelters. This means they do not euthanize healthy, behaviorally sound animals. But they may turn animals away if the shelter is full.

WHAT CAN VOLUNTEERS DO?

No matter the kind of shelter, there are many volunteer opportunities available. Some tasks involve working with animals directly. Some tasks are suitable for younger volunteers, and some are done mostly by adults. Young volunteers can help socialize the animals. Shelters can be stressful places for animals, including cats. By being

Taking shelter dogs for walks is essential to helping reduce stress in the animals.

nearby and playing with cats, volunteers make the cats more comfortable. They help the cats build trust. This makes the cats more likely to be adopted.

For older volunteers, walking dogs is another key job. Being cooped up in a kennel can be stressful. Going for walks can help relieve that stress. Volunteers can help train and groom dogs too. They can fill up bowls with food or water. They can help out by driving animals to veterinary appointments.

Some volunteer tasks do not involve working with animals. But they are still very important. It takes a lot to keep a shelter running smoothly. Many of these tasks are suitable for volunteers of all ages. Staff may need help with laundry. They may need help keeping the grounds tidy.

Some volunteers help keep kennel areas clean.

A shelter may have a store that sells pet supplies. Volunteers may be needed as cashiers. Nonprofit shelters may need to raise money. Volunteers can write or take

Taking good photos of shelter animals is important to helping them get adopted.

photos for flyers. They can post on social

media. They can help plan adoption events.

Two young women named Chloe and

Nona volunteer at Butte Humane Society in

California. They help out as photographers.

In an interview, they said, "It's so fun to try and capture their personalities in photos so that people who are looking to adopt can see who the pups really are. . . . We love being able to make an impact, no matter how small or large, in the shelter dogs' lives."[1]

BENEFITS OF VOLUNTEERING

Volunteering at an animal shelter has many benefits. Volunteers can see positive outcomes from their work. A dog's behavior improves over time. A cat becomes less shy around people. And eventually the animals go to good homes.

For the volunteer, this kind of work builds new skills. Some of those skills are specific to animals. This can help prepare the person for a future career. Other skills will help in any area of life. These include responsibility and the ability to manage time. Volunteering also improves a résumé or job application. It shows that a person has developed skills that would make her a good employee. It also shows that the person is passionate about a cause she believes in.

Volunteering at an animal shelter can be healthful too. Studies have shown that being with animals may reduce stress. It may

lower blood pressure. Some tasks, such as

walking dogs, can be good exercise.

GETTING INVOLVED

Most people can find an animal shelter

near them. There are about 5,000 of these

shelters in the United States. However, there

SHELTER NAMES

Two major animal rights groups are the Humane Society of the United States (HSUS) and the American Society for the Prevention of Cruelty to Animals (ASPCA). The HSUS does not operate any shelters. The ASPCA operates only one. Many local shelters have "humane society" or "SPCA" in their names, but they are not connected to these groups. Any shelter can use those terms in its name.

are some things people should keep in mind before volunteering.

Different shelters have different requirements for volunteers. There may be age requirements for certain tasks. There may be a time commitment, such as one year of weekly shifts. Depending on the task, there may be physical requirements too. People may need to stand for a long time, lift heavy objects, or operate machinery.

Volunteers should also think about what kind of shelter is right for them. Some people may prefer a no-kill shelter.

Animals in shelters may be scared. It is important to be patient and calm with them.

Those with allergies may need to avoid

shelters with certain animals. People should

be sure to research the shelter before

applying. A volunteer should also make

sure that they can emotionally handle the

shelter environment. A shelter can be noisy.

The animals may not be well-behaved.

Volunteers have to be patient. Animals

are often very stressed. It can also be

hard seeing the ways animals have been

mistreated. But for many animal lovers,

helping the animals find loving homes

makes it all worth it.

When a person decides to apply, there

is some paperwork involved. She needs

to fill out an application form. This may be

a paper form or online. Shelters may also

require a volunteer to sign a waiver. This

protects the shelter legally if a volunteer

Volunteers may need to be taught certain training methods before working with dogs.

gets hurt. Once a person applies and

is accepted, there is usually a training

process. Volunteers learn their way around

the shelter. They learn the proper way to do

their tasks.

CHAPTER TWO

HOW CAN I VOLUNTEER AT A WILDLIFE CENTER?

Wildlife centers take in wild animals that are orphaned, injured, or sick. They care for the animals, helping them grow or heal. This work is called rehabilitation. The ultimate goal is to release the animals back into the wild.

Wildlife centers provide medical care to injured or sick wild animals.

Some animals are no longer able to survive in the wild. They may be euthanized or kept in captivity for educational purposes.

People should not try to care for wild animals on their own. Wildlife centers

People at wildlife centers make sure animals are gaining or maintaining weight, depending on the animal's needs.

have the experts and facilities to do this work properly and safely. They must get state and federal licenses to do this important work. This ensures that they are rehabilitating animals the right way.

Wildlife centers work with many kinds of animals. They may help birds, bats, porcupines, turtles, foxes, and many others. The variety depends on the time of year and the part of the country. For example, the Wildlife Rehabilitation Center of Minnesota recorded more than 180 **species** in a single year.

Wildlife centers often rely on donations and fundraising to operate. They typically have a staff of full-time workers. These include veterinarians who care for animals. Other staff oversee the volunteers.

Some large centers may use hundreds of volunteers.

WHAT CAN VOLUNTEERS DO?

Veterinarians handle the treatment of wild animals, but there are many tasks for volunteers too. One of the biggest tasks is cleaning. This not only makes the center look nicer but also provides a better environment for the growing and healing animals. Volunteers clean cages and food dishes. They run loads of laundry to keep bedding and towels clean. They mop floors indoors and clean pools for waterfowl

Orphaned babies may need to be bottle-fed at a wildlife center.

outdoors. They also make sure the hospital spaces are safe and sanitary.

Volunteers can work directly with the animals too. Some of these tasks are limited to adults. But volunteers under age eighteen can do some of these things if adults are with them. One such task may be caring for ducklings. The Wildlife Rehabilitation Center of Minnesota takes in orphaned ducklings. The center raises them so that they can survive in the wild.

At the center, volunteers feed the ducklings fish and insects. They make sure the supplies in the duckling area are fully stocked. Volunteers also use hoses and brushes to keep the duckling enclosures clean. As the ducklings grow, they move to a larger outdoor space. This is their last stop before being released into the wild. Volunteers continue to feed the birds.

Volunteers may clean the pool for ducklings at a wildlife center.

They closely follow instructions from the

center's staff.

There are other ways for volunteers to

help wildlife centers. They can write for

social media and newsletters. They can

work on the center's website, and they can help out at fundraising events. People can volunteer on the phone too. Members of the public may call the center when they find an animal that needs help. Volunteers can pass along the message to the appropriate expert.

BENEFITS OF VOLUNTEERING

For animal lovers, wildlife center volunteering can be very rewarding. Volunteers can watch the animals grow and heal over time. They can clearly see the results of their work. By helping animals return to the wild, they are helping local **ecosystems**.

Over time volunteers may become

attached to an animal they are helping. They

must be careful that the animal doesn't

bond too closely with them. That would

make it harder for the animal to survive in

the wild later. But some wildlife centers give

HABITUATION

One of the most important things at a wildlife center is avoiding habituation. This happens when an animal bonds too closely to the humans taking care of it. It gets used to a human presence. This can harm its chances of survival in the wild. Wild animals are naturally fearful of people. To avoid habituation, volunteers should not talk to animals. Centers try to keep human contact with the animals to a minimum.

volunteers the chance to personally release animals back into the wild. This can make the experience even more satisfying.

Amanda Margraves is a wildlife rehabilitator. She works at the Florida Keys Wild Bird Rehabilitation Center. She described this part of the job: "The most rewarding part of this job is to watch a healed animal be released back into the wild where they belong."[2]

Volunteering at wildlife centers can prepare people for future careers. They may have an interest in working as full-time staff members at a center. They may want

Some animals at a wildlife center can no longer survive in the wild due to injuries, such as to the eyes or wings.

to help wildlife as a job. Volunteering can

give them a window into that experience.

Margraves gives this advice to people

interested in a rehabilitation career:

"Volunteer! Start by volunteering at a local

wildlife center. . . . Volunteering helps [people] get experience and they can figure out if they really want to rehab."[3]

GETTING INVOLVED

There are a few things people should keep in mind when considering wildlife center volunteering. First, the tasks and animals that people can work with often depend on the age of the volunteer. Young volunteers may need to work alongside a parent or guardian. Teens ages sixteen or seventeen may be able to volunteer alone, but they may not be able to work with more difficult animals. Volunteers ages eighteen or over can usually work with almost all animals.

But they may need a rabies vaccine to work

with animals that can spread that disease.

Volunteers should consider physical

requirements too. They may need to stand

for a long time. They may need to walk on

wet, slippery floors. They may need to lift

RABIES

Rabies is a disease caused by a virus. It can infect wildlife, including skunks, raccoons, and bats. Those animals can then spread the disease to people by biting them. Rabies is extremely dangerous. It almost always leads to death, though people can be saved if they get to a doctor and get rabies shots right away. As a result, wildlife centers are very careful with species that may carry rabies.

Volunteering at a wildlife center can be rewarding.

and carry things. Volunteers might need to feed animals. This could involve handling live fish or insects, so volunteers need to be comfortable with that. Finally, volunteers should be aware of the commitment they are making. They may need to sign up for a certain number of weekly shifts. It is important to follow through on this commitment.

CHAPTER THREE

HOW CAN I VOLUNTEER AS A CITIZEN SCIENTIST?

Citizen science involves everyday people helping out with scientific projects. These people work as volunteers. They make observations and gather data, often near where they live. This helps scientists get information over a wide

A school class might participate in a citizen science project.

area. It lets them do more research with less money. Many citizen science projects involve animals.

All kinds of people can get involved in citizen science. Volunteers might be children studying animals in their local parks. They might be members of high school science clubs taking field trips to study wetlands. They might be adult **birders** who observe animals as a hobby.

No matter who is involved, citizen science can help animals. The information

THE CHRISTMAS BIRD COUNT

One of the first citizen science projects dates back to 1900. In that year the National Audubon Society started the Christmas Bird Count. From December 14 to January 5 each year, groups of people around North America collect data about local bird populations. The project is still going today. There are more than 2,000 local groups that participate across the United States and Canada.

people gather is sent to scientists

and **conservationists**. It may be used to

plan conservation projects. Citizen scientists

can play an important role in protecting

ecosystems and the animals that live there.

WHAT CAN VOLUNTEERS DO?

There are a wide variety of citizen science

projects around the country. They involve

different kinds of animals and different sets

of skills. Volunteers can find opportunities

that match their interests.

One common type of citizen science

project is known as a BioBlitz. In this event,

volunteers identify species in a particular

area. Many volunteers work together to find as many species as they can in a short period of time. The area may be small, such as a single backyard. Or it may be large, covering a whole country. Events may last anywhere from a few hours to a few weeks.

Volunteers can record their notes on paper, but smartphones can make the process easier. BioBlitz apps make it simple to take down a lot of data quickly. Volunteers can include photos, video clips, and sound recordings with their notes. They upload this information to a database so scientists can use it.

Smartphone apps can make it easy to record data for citizen science projects.

BioBlitz volunteers work to answer many different questions. How many species are in the area? Which ones are the most common? Besides adult animals, are there things such as eggs and larvae?

How are people affecting the area that is being studied? Answering these questions helps improve scientists' understanding of the environment.

Another citizen science project is called NestWatch. It is run by the Cornell Lab of Ornithology. Volunteers search for bird nests in their local areas. They watch the nests over time. They take notes on when birds lay eggs, how many they lay, and how many hatch. Volunteers record all this information on an app or website. Researchers can then use that data to learn more about bird nesting patterns.

It is important to not disturb a nest when monitoring it.

Anyone can volunteer with NestWatch, but they must learn the right way to study nests. Birds often lay eggs in the morning, so people should visit nests later in the day. People should be careful not to leave tracks

Because frogs' skin easily absorbs toxins, their numbers can tell scientists if there is a problem with their habitats.

to the nests. Predators might follow the footprints. Volunteers should never touch the eggs or young birds. Finally, volunteers should always ask permission before studying nests on private land.

A similar citizen science project is called FrogWatch USA. The Association of Zoos and Aquariums runs this program. People around the country receive training on frogs and toads. They learn to identify the calls of these animals in their own areas. They write down observations about what they hear. The project helps scientists learn more about how frog populations change over time.

BENEFITS OF VOLUNTEERING

Citizen science projects have benefits for scientists. They help scientists gather more data than they could otherwise. With the help of citizen scientists, one researcher can get data from thousands of places around the country. Information from programs such as NestWatch has been used in scientific studies. Citizen science also strengthens connections between scientists and their local communities.

These projects have benefits for the volunteers too. People get to enjoy spending time in nature. If they are volunteering with a group, they may be able to work alongside their friends. They also get a chance to learn how the scientific process works. Learning to observe animals and collect data can help prepare volunteers for a career in science.

Citizen science projects such as tagging monarch butterflies help scientists monitor wildlife populations.

Finally, citizen science also benefits

the environment. Scientists are able to

use the data to plan future conservation

projects. Knowing how animal populations

are changing may help scientists identify

problems to solve. Getting people

CITIZEN SCIENCE COMPETITION

Some citizen science projects use competition to motivate volunteers. In 2016 two museums in California held BioBlitz events. One was in Los Angeles, and the other was in San Francisco. They competed to find as many species as they could. More than 1,000 people participated. They made more than 20,000 observations. They even found some species that hadn't been seen in these areas before. In later years, more cities around the world joined the competition.

interested in conservation is a benefit too. Environmentalist Juan Martinez explained how BioBlitzes can help in this way. He said, "If we get more people to think of themselves as explorers and protectors and conservationists of this world, it'll be a better world."[4]

GETTING INVOLVED

There are many ways to get involved in citizen science. These programs may be organized through schools or youth groups. They are also hosted by museums, zoos, and nature centers. If people can't find any

Binoculars can make it easier to identify different kinds of birds at a distance.

local programs, they may be able to find citizen science projects online.

Depending on the project, a person might need some basic equipment. Binoculars can be useful for studying birds. Digital microscopes let people see microorganisms. Nets help people catch insects. Smartphones provide a way to record observations and upload them to a database. The organization running the program may provide the needed equipment.

CHAPTER FOUR

HOW CAN I VOLUNTEER AT A ZOO?

There are thousands of zoos around the world. Zoos let visitors see animals from faraway places. Visitors can learn about these animals. They can also learn about conservation efforts. Zoos often help protect animals in their natural habitats.

Zoos can be great places to educate people about conservation.

Zoos are staffed by professional zookeepers. These experts know how to care for animals. They have learned how to keep themselves and the animals safe. Each zookeeper may focus on one type of animal. For example, one may work with birds and another with fish. Zookeepers work alongside scientists and other professionals to run a zoo.

Zoos also have many volunteer opportunities. Some of these opportunities are only for people over eighteen. They

ISSUES WITH ZOOS

Zoos are sometimes **controversial**. Some people criticize them for not taking care of animals properly. They may believe it is wrong to keep wild animals in captivity. Zoo supporters believe that zoos have a valuable role in education. They believe that seeing animals in person can inspire guests to support conservation. They think that well-run zoos take good care of their animals.

may come with a lot of responsibility or training. But younger teens can find many opportunities too. Sometimes they can volunteer on their own. In other cases they can volunteer alongside a parent or guardian.

WHAT CAN VOLUNTEERS DO?

One key volunteer position at zoos is ambassador. This position may also be called greeter. Ambassadors welcome guests who come to the zoo. They share information and help guests find their way around. For example, they might explain the schedule for a bird or reptile show. Or they might explain where to find the zebras or the penguins. They may also share the history of the zoo.

Sue is an ambassador volunteer at the Saint Louis Zoo in Missouri. She said, "We are the meet and greet arm of the Zoo. It is so interesting meeting people from all over the country—and even the world." She added, "Visitors appreciate our help in giving directions to animals."[5]

A similar volunteer position is a docent. At some zoos these might even be the same role. Docents may also show guests around. But they often help educate

At some zoos, volunteer docents may be able to help the public safely interact with certain animals.

guests too. They learn about the animals at

the zoo. Then they share that information

with guests. They may also teach guests

about the zoo's conservation work.

A common volunteer opportunity for

teens is helping out with day camps.

Many zoos run these programs for young kids. The kids stay at the zoo all day and do activities, games, and lessons. They learn about the zoo and its animals. Adult staff members are in charge of these programs. Teen volunteers help the adults. They make sure the day camp runs smoothly. Volunteers may help during check-in and checkout. They may help set up activities and games. They help the day campers learn and stay safe.

Volunteers usually do not work with animals. The professional zookeepers have the training to do this safely. However, there are some opportunities for volunteers to be with animals. Some zoos have a petting zoo section. Volunteers may care for these animals. They watch guests and make sure the animals are safe. Zoos may have butterfly houses. These are rooms where many butterflies can fly freely. Guests can enjoy looking at the colorful insects.

THE IMPORTANCE OF VOLUNTEERS

Zoos are popular places to volunteer. Volunteers can make a big difference at the zoos where they work. For example, the Saint Louis Zoo uses volunteers for many roles. Each year, the zoo's volunteers serve for more than 100,000 hours in all.

Just like with the petting zoo, volunteers make sure guests are following the rules.

BENEFITS OF VOLUNTEERING

Volunteering at a zoo is very helpful if a person is interested in a zookeeping career. Volunteers can learn more about what working at a zoo is like. They may discover what kinds of animals they want to work with. Volunteers can talk to zoo staff to learn more about career options.

Zoo volunteers also help with conservation efforts. They educate the public about wildlife and the ways people can protect it. This may inspire members

Many zoos have captive breeding programs. They breed endangered species such as pandas so the species do not go extinct.

of the public to support conservation. They

may donate to conservation causes. Or

they may vote with conservation in mind.

Education can make a big difference.

For people who love animals, volunteering at the zoo may be its own reward. They get to spend time near all kinds of animals. They can share their passion for nature with zoo guests. One volunteer at the Maryland Zoo said, "You've engaged, you've had fun, you've laughed. You can't come here and not be happy by the time you leave."[6] Volunteers can learn more about wildlife and conservation. They may also get a discount at zoo gift shops.

GETTING INVOLVED

Volunteering at a zoo begins with sending in an application. There may be an

Zoo volunteers typically need to have some training.

interview too. The zoo staff wants to make

sure the volunteer is right for the role. After a

volunteer is accepted, there may be training

or an orientation. Volunteers learn more

about the work. They meet with staff and

fellow volunteers.

Zoo volunteering often requires a commitment. People may need to commit to a certain number of hours per year. If they are interacting with guests, volunteers should have a positive attitude. They should be knowledgeable about the zoo and its exhibits.

HELPING ANIMALS

There are many ways to volunteer for animal welfare. Some people care for homeless pets. Others help treat injured wildlife. Volunteers can study local wildlife to help conservation programs. Or they can educate the public at zoos. They can help

Anyone can help raise awareness about the threats animals face today.

people get excited about animals. They can inspire others to help with conservation.

All of these options help the volunteer too. Volunteers can learn more about animals. They can prepare for future careers. They can gain valuable skills and demonstrate responsibility. And they can simply enjoy working with animals.

GLOSSARY

birders

people whose hobby is observing birds in the wild

conservationists

people who protect the environment and the plants and animals in it

controversial

causing opposing views

ecosystems

specific areas and the living things found in them

euthanize

to kill a sick or injured animal in a way that minimizes pain

kennels

containers that hold animals

species

specific types of living things

SOURCE NOTES

CHAPTER ONE: HOW CAN I VOLUNTEER AT AN ANIMAL SHELTER?

1. Quoted in "Volunteer Spotlight Interview: Chloe and Nona," *Butte Humane Society*, 2021. https://buttehumane.org.

CHAPTER TWO: HOW CAN I VOLUNTEER AT A WILDLIFE CENTER?

2. Quoted in Korrie Edwards, "Interview with Amanda Margraves: Head Wildlife Rehabilitator," *Green Mind Initiative* (blog), *WordPress*, June 5, 2015. https://thegreenmindinitiative.wordpress.com.

3. Quoted in Edwards, "Interview with Amanda Margraves: Head Wildlife Rehabilitator."

CHAPTER THREE: HOW CAN I VOLUNTEER AS A CITIZEN SCIENTIST?

4. Quoted in "BioBlitz 2016 Introduction," *National Geographic Education*, *YouTube*, April 18, 2016. www.youtube.com.

CHAPTER FOUR: HOW CAN I VOLUNTEER AT A ZOO?

5. Quoted in "Volunteer: Ambassadors," *Saint Louis Zoo*, 2021. www.stlzoo.org.

6. Quoted in "About Volunteering," *Maryland Zoo*, 2021. www.marylandzoo.org.

FOR FURTHER RESEARCH

BOOKS

John Hamilton, *Raptor Rescue*. Minneapolis, MN: Abdo, 2018.

Kathryn Hulick, *Citizen Science: How Anyone Can Contribute to Scientific Discovery*. San Diego, CA: ReferencePoint Press, 2020.

INTERNET SOURCES

"Citizen Science Projects," *National Geographic*, 2021. www.nationalgeographic.org.

"Volunteering," *Seattle Humane*, 2021. www.seattlehumane.org.

WEBSITES

American Association of Zoos and Aquariums (AZA)
www.aza.org

The AZA is a national organization of zoos and aquariums in the United States. It ensures its members have high standards of animal welfare and helps with conservation and research.

CitizenScience.gov
www.citizenscience.gov

This US government website features information about citizen science projects with federal agencies. Many of these projects involve animals and the environment.

RELATED ORGANIZATIONS

American Humane

1400 16th St. NW, Suite 360
Washington, DC 20036
info@americanhumane.org
www.americanhumane.org

American Humane is a major animal welfare organization in the United States. It helps rescue animals in danger, ensures animals are safe on movie sets, and works for humane treatment of farm animals. American Humane does not operate local shelters, though shelters often use the word *humane* in their names. People should contact local shelters about volunteer opportunities near them.

Smithsonian's National Zoo

3001 Connecticut Ave. NW
Washington, DC 20008
https://nationalzoo.si.edu

The Smithsonian's National Zoo is located in the US capital, Washington, DC. Its website includes information about the many volunteer opportunities there. Zoos around the nation have their own volunteer programs. Each has its own opportunities and set of requirements. People interested in volunteering should contact their local zoo to learn about the opportunities available.

INDEX

age requirements, 18, 24, 33, 40, 62–63, 65–66
American Society for the Prevention of Cruelty to Animals (ASPCA), 23
animal shelters, 6–11, 12–27
applications, 11, 22, 25–27, 70
Association of Zoos and Aquariums, 52–53

BioBlitz, 47–49, 56, 57
butterfly houses, 67

careers, 11, 22, 38–39, 54, 68, 73
Christmas Bird Count, 46
citizen science, 11, 44–59
cleaning, 9, 32, 34
conservation, 47, 56–57, 60, 62, 65, 68–70, 72–73

day camps, 65–66

ecosystems, 36, 47

FrogWatch USA, 52
fundraising, 19, 31, 36

habituation, 37
health benefits, 22–23
Humane Society of the United States (HSUS), 23

laundry, 8–9, 18, 32

Margraves, Amanda, 38–39
Martinez, Juan, 57
Maryland Zoo, 70

NestWatch, 50–51, 54

petting zoos, 67–68
photography, 20–21

rabies, 41

Saint Louis Zoo, 64, 67
skills, 11, 22, 47, 73
social media, 20, 35
stress, 14, 16, 18, 23, 26

training, 27, 53, 63, 66, 71

wildlife rehabilitation centers, 11, 28–43

zoo ambassador, 63–64
zoo docent, 64
zookeepers, 61–62, 66
zoos, 11, 57, 60–72

IMAGE CREDITS

ABOUT THE AUTHOR

Walt K. Moon is a writer who lives in Minnesota. He enjoys volunteering at his local library.